Dedicated to my Barbara and her Beautiful mother

2

Presentation

How to start in the search for Treasures? Basic information for beginners is a book that aims to teach the most basic but useful concepts to develop this activity.

The focus of this book is for people who do not have any experience in the subject but want to start.

Without technical information, incomprehensible to the reader, this book contains everything a beginner needs as well for people who have just started in the search.

Basic concepts, search tips and security are the three basic topics that can be found in this text.

Enjoy it.

Introduction

The search for treasures is a generally recreational activity that is taking a lot of force in our society, being a relatively new activity is not enough experience or information about the search for treasures, which generates many doubts to those who start this hobby.

This text tries to show us in a very practical way the basic foundations of treasure detection with the aim of not starting this activity without knowledge, it is not intended to give technical information that hinders learning but more colloquial information with technical support and well-founded that will facilitate the initiation in this hobby.

The compilation of empirical experience of thousands of amateurs and professionals, specialized texts and information data from large companies have helped us to give truth to this small book of induction into the wonderful world of treasure hunts.

Excellent text for people without previous knowledge about treasure detection.

Index

Preface

What are the most frequent questions of those people who do not know about treasure detection?

What is prospection?

What is a treasure?

Is it legal?

How deep is the detector?

These are some of the questions in which the answer will be found in this text.

You already know the basics, it's time to start looking, but where? There are other answers that also have an answer in this little book.

We can not forget security, a very important issue in the search for treasures that can not go unnoticed by anyone who is dedicated to this activity, much less for who is their first experience.

These are the three basic themes that have been expressed in the book, which will make it easier for you to start out in search of treasures.

The author.

Concepts and basic questions

9

What is the treasure hunt?

The treasure hunt is an outdoor activity (mainly) where, with the help of a metal detector, metallic objects of buried value are searched, this activity is also called prospection, in this activity you can find coins, jewelery , relics and many metal objects, some with a great historical value, some with a great monetary value.

10

What is a treasure?

A treasure is the discovery of one or several objects of commercial and historical value, whether gold, silver, relics, jewelry or any other object that is attractive to be marketed in the market or with collectors and that has time buried underground.

Is it legal?

The search for treasures is a completely legal activity and is based on the federal laws of our country (Mexico) where, in a very general way, it tells us the following:

- Hidden treasures are not any fruit of any property therefore they do not have an owner.

- If you find some treasure in the property or land of your property, it is yours.

- If you find some treasure on the property or property of a third party there are two options.

  - If you have your permission, it is divided by halves.

12

- o If you do not have your permission, the owner of the property or land can claim the treasure found and request the repair of the damage caused to the property

- If the treasure is of interest to science or culture or the arts, the government can expropriate it through a fair payment.

The articles that support this list can be found in the bibliography.

In your country maybe there is a law too.

What is a metal detector?

It is a search instrument for metallic items whose main purpose is the location of hidden treasures in land and farms, it is also used to find lost objects such as beaches.

There are two types of detectors, very low frequency detectors (VLF) and pulse induction detectors (PI).

There are many types of detectors with different functions, which range from a simple sound signal as soon as they detect a metal, a depth indicator of the object, type of probable object, to the graph of the same object found in 3D.

VLF Detector

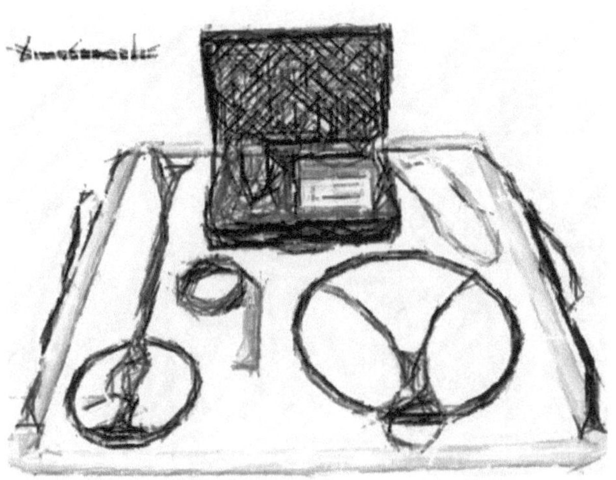

PI Detector

How do metal detectors work?

The great majority of the detectors work in the following way, inside the plate has two coils, one of them is responsible for generating an electromagnetic field that penetrates through the ground and as soon as it detects a metal the signal is distorted.

The second coil is in charge of receiving that distortion that is later analyzed by the microcomputer of the detector, is analyzed and sends a tone to indicate that a metal has been detected.

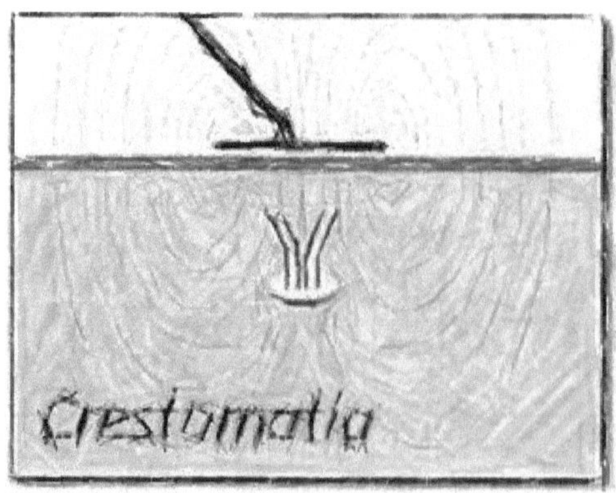

16

What is the coil or plate?

The coils or plate is the disc at the end of the detector's stem, it is responsible for emitting and receiving the electromagnetic signal within the search area, there are several types of coils or plates, as well as different sizes.

Coil types

Crestomatía

Circular or concentric: This coil gives us slightly more depth of detection and detectability in non-mineralized soils, this is the coil most used in metal detectors.

Crestomatía

Elliptical: It is the most manageable and its width offers a greater coverage than the circular one.

17

2 Boxes: They are used to detect buried objects at great depths.

Crestomatía

Double "D": This coil is designed to significantly reduce ground interference, this allows you to recover the performance with respect to a circular or concentric coil on a mineralized ground.

18

What is discrimination?

It is one of the main characteristics of a detector, this function refers to the ability to reject an objective by the detector based on its metallic composition and electrical conductivity.

Important. When you are starting to search for treasures is not recommended to discriminate any object, until you have sufficient experience, often treasures are hidden in containers that a detector can mark as ferrous.

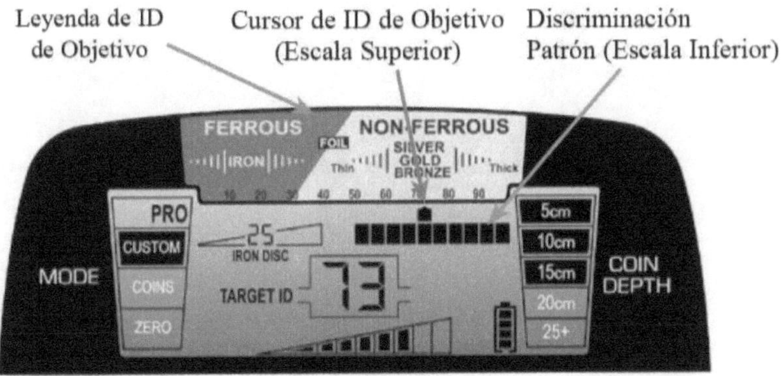

How deep is a detector?

The depth of a detector depends on a number of factors and one of them is mainly the size and type of the coil or disk, which as a general rule, will be approximately equal to its diameter, for an object the size of a coin or small object

However, as the size of the scanning coil increases and its field pattern enlarges, the field pattern becomes less concentrated and begins not to detect small objects.

20

Factors that modify the Depth of a detector

1. The type of metal detector: The technology used for detection is the biggest factor in the detector's capacity.
2. The type of metal in the object: Some metals, such as steel, create stronger magnetic fields and are easier to detect..
3. The size of the object: A can of soda has a surface wider than a coin to be detected.
4. Position of the object: It has more detection area an object whose surface is in horizontal position than one of the same size in vertical position.
5. The composition of the earth: Certain minerals are natural conductors and can cause serious interferences in the metal detector.
6. The halo of the object: When certain types of metals that have been buried for long periods of time, they can increase the conductivity of the earth around them.
7. Interference from other objects: These items may be on the ground, such as cables,

pipes, or above ground, such as high-voltage lines and other detectors.

8. Discrimination: The use of this function in the detectors decreases the depth capacity, since when discriminating we are subtracting power from the detector.

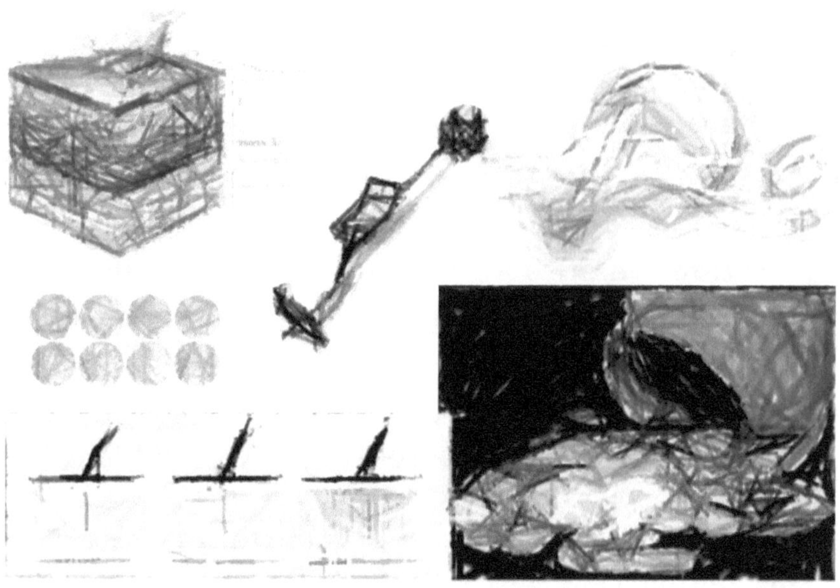

What are ferrous and non-ferrous objects?

Ferrous Objects: Are all metals whose base is iron

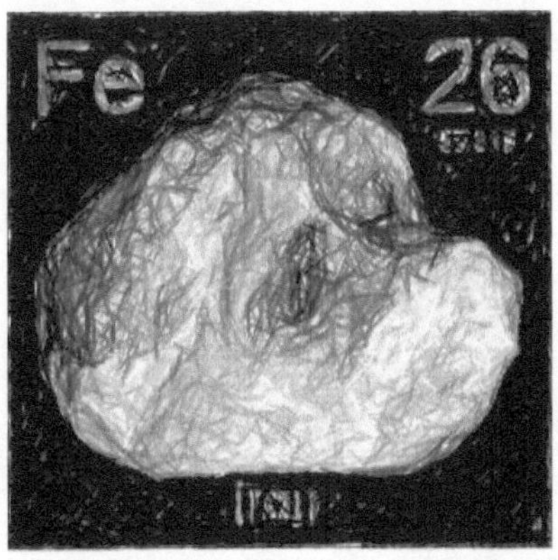

Non-Ferrous Objects: Are those metals and alloys that do not contain iron in their composition, in general they are soft and have little resistance, among the most important are copper, zinc, lead, tin, aluminum, nickel and manganese.

23

Gold, silver and platinum are the only metals that do not contain iron and are not created based on an alloy of metals.

The following illustration shows some of these metals and the use that is given to each one of them.

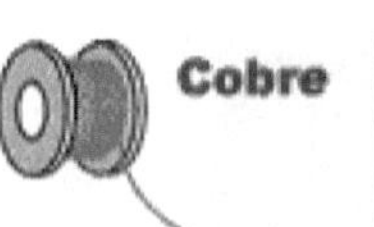

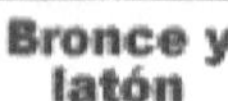

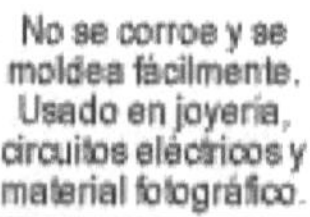

What is the Object ID?

In a metal detector, it is the number that shows us from 1 to 99 regularly, this is no more than the graphic indication of the probable identity of the target based on its electrical conduction properties.

In the following table, some identifications of objects are shown based on the number shown by the detector

Object	Id. Numeric	Observations
The majority of ferrous objects	4-12	
Aluminum foil chewing gum	16-25	
Nickel from the USA ($ 0.05 coin)	30	Typically
Aluminum boat slip	33-55	

25

Bolt-on aluminum bottle cap	60-70	
Zinc currency (penny date after 1982)	60	Typically
Aluminum can for soda	63-69	Very often, but it can vary a lot
Copper pennies, coated	70	Typically
25 cents american peseta	80	Typically
Modern 50 Cent Coin	86	Typically
Silver dollar coin, ancient	90	Typically
USA Eagle silver coin, $ 1	91	Typically
Table 1. Objects ID		

Bank tests

This is a very important step before going out to look for our treasures as it is our first experience with the detector and a metal.

1. What you have to do in this step is turn on our detector in a place clear of metals or electrical source that may affect the detector.
2. Select different metals (gold, silver, aluminum, copper, etc) that we have at our disposal.
3. Pass each metal in front of the coil of our detector and identify the tone it produces, the ID that shows on our screen as well as see which segment appears on our detector.

This step gives us a lot of information about how the detector behaves with the metals that we find, very useful information because when we are in the field and we see a signal similar to the one already identified in the bank tests, we will have an idea of what we are finding.

27

MAPA 2. Zonas controladas por los caudillos cristeros (1926-1929)

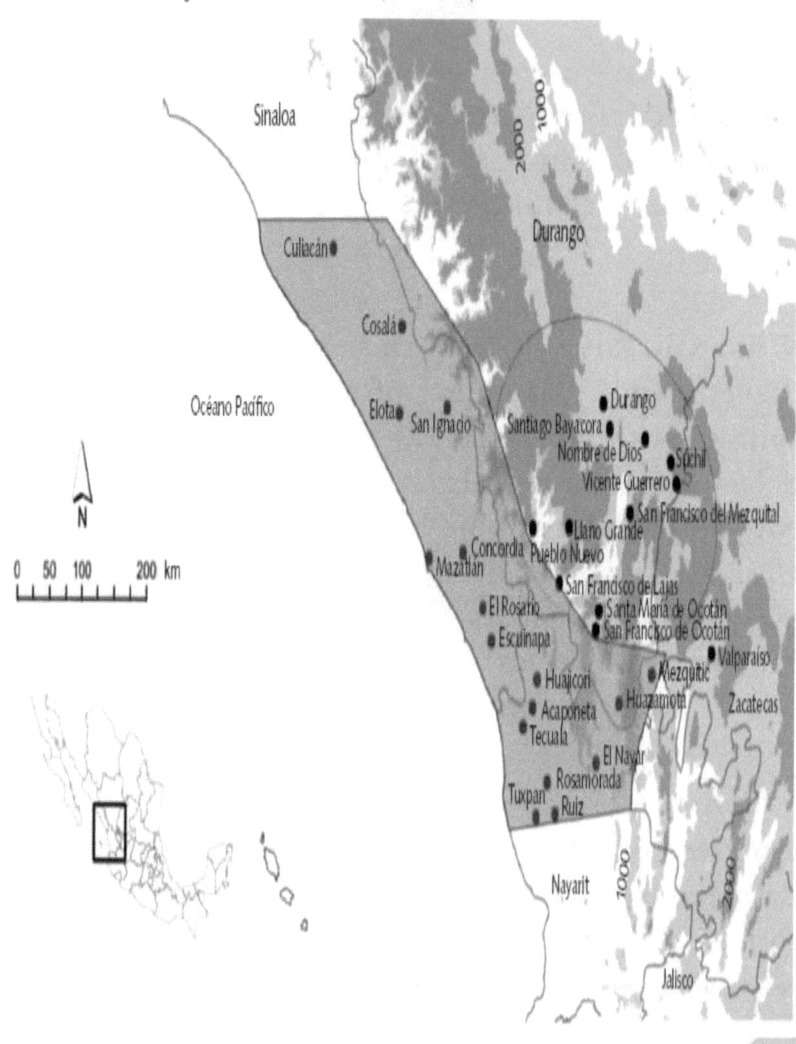

28

Mas de 900 años de historia tiene el tesoro de L5, ubicado y confirmado, jamás encontrado
L:19.67 L: -99.17 2017

L5 - Treasure

Where to Look?

Irving Jorge Galindo Salto

30

When you acquire your detector and you have not defined a place to look, here we can recommend some places to start looking.

Open field: There are many places to start the search, it can be the garden of the house, some park, fields, real roads, etc., there are many areas that used to be wagon passes where they developed and were the scenarios of many battles or assaults, in all those places many treasures were lost, it is indispensable to study the history of the land to have greater certainty.

31

Farms: With the development of wars and great battles through time there was much looting and robbery on the part of the guerrillas in addition to the fact that banks did not exist, people in search of not stealing their wealth opted to hide their treasures in the less inhospitable places, with time the people died and the treasures were forgotten, then a series of places where treasures have been found are listed.Paredes

- Pig Farms
- Latrines
- Stables

Beaches: One of the places where people lose many objects during their vacations, it is recommended to look for during and after holiday periods.

Wells: The people who hid the treasures in these cavities threw it to the bottom, descended through it and at a certain depth into a horizontal hole (like a safe behind a painting) where it kept what it wanted to hide, so it is advisable to look around of the well, not on it.

33

Trees burned by lightning: The burnt trees are a good sign to find silver, there is a great chance of finding it at its roots because silver is an excellent conductor of electricity, but do not forget to make sure very well with your detector.

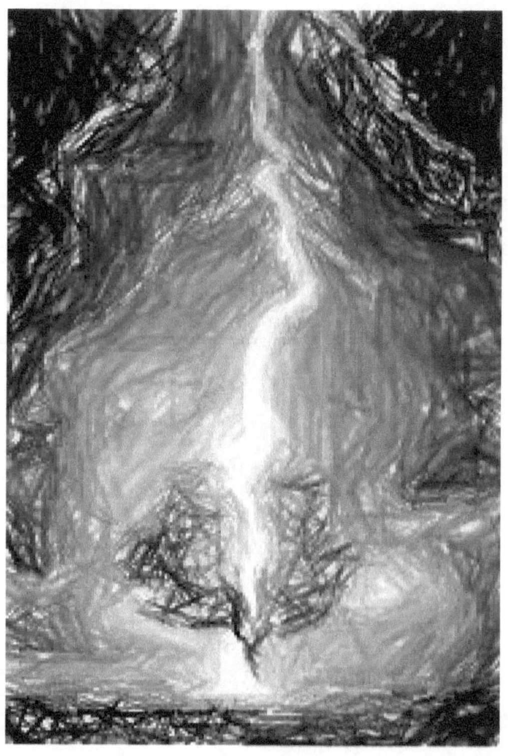

34

Skirts of Hills: Because of their distance in previous times from the center of the cities, these places were the preferred ones by the bandits to hide their stolen treasures, this makes them an excellent place to conduct surveys.

Basic information for the search

Irving Jorge Galindo Salto

36

Before starting the search you have to perform the bench tests and work the detector with the default settings that the detector brings during the first 10 hours, this time is for you to become familiar with the detector, performance, brands, etc.

How deep are the treasures?

There is a false belief that the treasures are buried very deep, although if there are some deep, most of them are very shallow it ranges between 0.80 (2.5 feets) and 1.40 (4.6 feets) meters for objects such as pitchers, jugs, chests, etc. The depth of coins and loose pieces are usually not more than 30 (11.8 inches) centimeters underground.

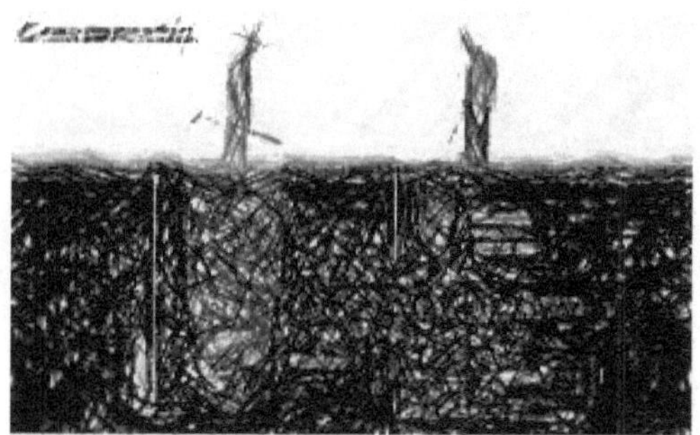

These depths are due to the fact that most of the people who hid their treasures did not have enough time and resources to hide it in greater depth, there were no banks and furthermore to dig deeper can be very difficult due to the different layers of the earth.

38

Meaning and way to look when you see it burn

Many people say that they have seen flares of different colors in different areas or places, this is a very good reason to acquire a detector but you must take into account that when you see burning you can usually see three types of coloring, this is because in the earth a crack opens and gas is released, which upon contact with oxygen generates the reaction, then what that color or light could mean is described.

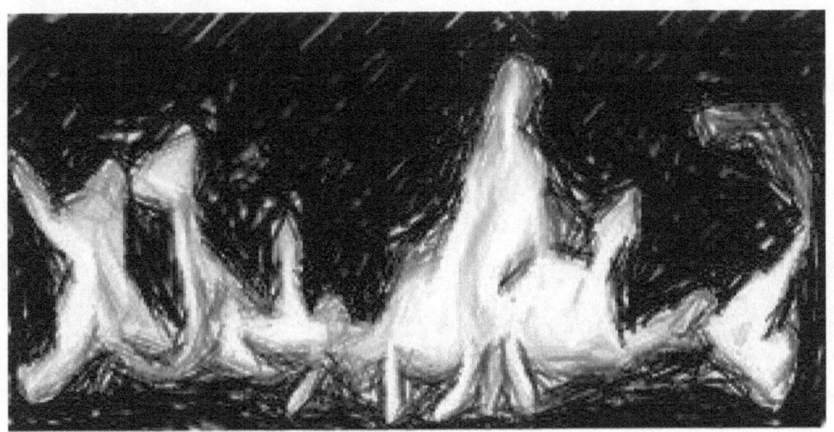

White light: This light is produced by the phosphorus produced by bones or silver, so you have a 50% chance of getting something good, verify very well that the detector indicates silver.

Reddish light: This light is produced by organic matter, mainly trees fallen many years ago and being buried, this light does not mean much probability of success.

Greenish blue light: This light is very similar to that seen when alcohol is consuming, when you see this light the probability of finding gold in coins or gold bars is high.

Once the color of the light was identified and it was decided to dig, the question arises: do I excavate exactly where the light appeared?

The answer to this question is no, just like the water when there is a leak, it looks for an exit and we see it not exactly where the leak occurred, so to be able to find the treasure we will have to start looking for where the light can be seen in spiral way to get a positive signal of the possible metal in our detector.

How to unearth a found treasure?

Once the treasure is found, it is time to start digging, for this you will need the following tool, Gloves, Talacho, Shovel, Pico.

For shallow objects it is recommended to do an excavation no larger than the diameter of the detector's disc, mark a circle and put the shovel to try to remove the entire block of earth, once the piece of earth is removed detector or a PinPointer (many of the detectors already include this function) to the pile of land to locate the object, the object is obtained and the hole is covered again.

Objects of great depth must be started little by little until they have an excavation with a diameter of no more than 2.5 meters (8.2 feets).

If the unearthed object is of great value it is recommended for safety to leave the place as soon as possible

42

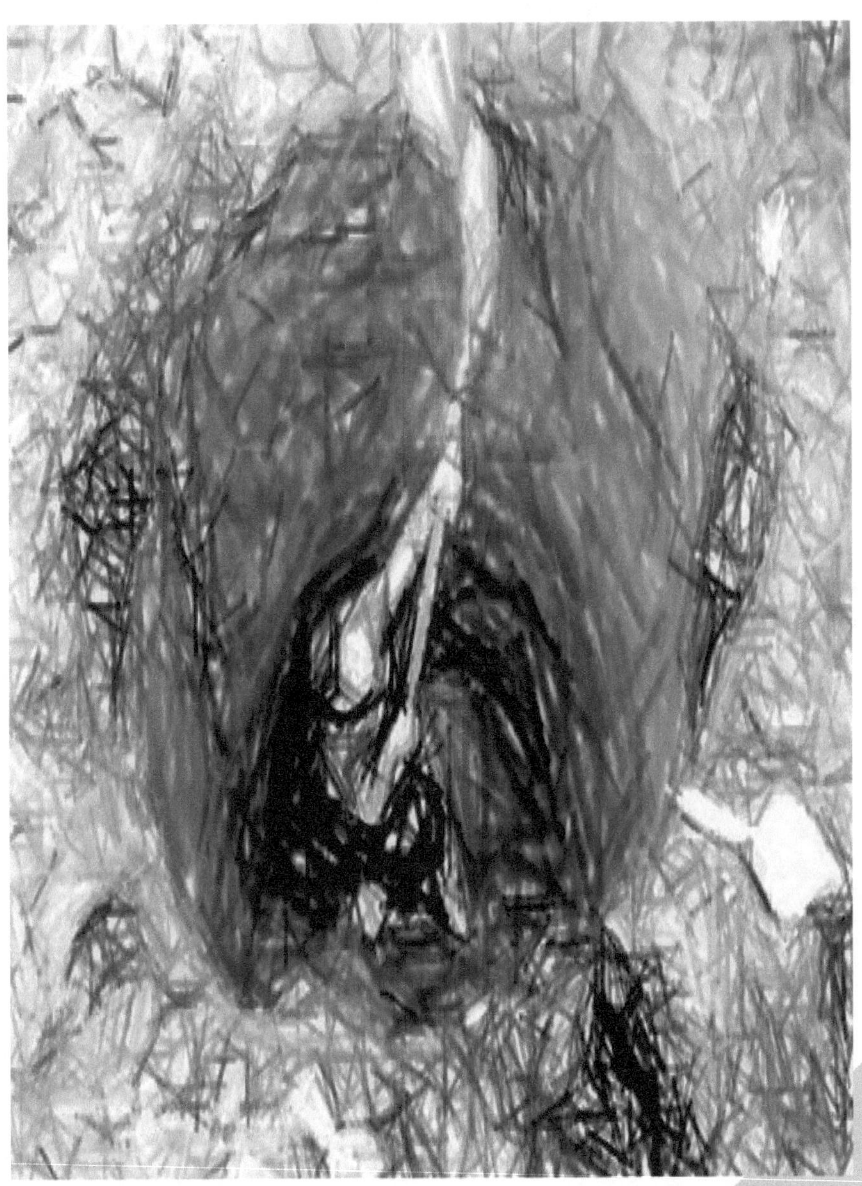

43

Irving Jorge Galindo Salto

Security Recommendations

Irving Jorge Galindo Salto

Hydrargirism - Mercury Poisoning

Hydrargirism is a disease or injury caused by the inhalation of mercury. Once it has been absorbed, it tends to accumulate in all living beings and is not discarded because, by its nature, it is not necessary to fulfill any kind of biological process.

Symptoms of Mercury poisoning

Characteristic symptoms are vomiting, difficulty breathing, intense cough, gum inflammation, loss of appetite with muscle weakness and a certain metallic taste.

When you get to inhale the mercury, it manifests itself through some symptoms that occur immediately when you inhale enough, producing an acute picture of intoxication.

If a significant amount of mercury is inhaled, it could cause long-term brain damage, permanent lung damage and even death.

If this happens, you should turn to a doctor or hospital as soon as possible.

46

Treatment of Mercury poisoning

In the case of elemental mercury inhalation poisoning, treatment can be difficult, but in this case the patient is given oxygen or humidified air sessions, and a breathing tube is placed inside the lungs. suck the mercury from the lungs, and is medicated with drugs that help remove heavy metals such as mercury from the body.

How to prevent poisoning

Much is said that you have to use vinegar because it contains acetic acid and this helps neutralize the effects of mercury, the fact is that this is not scientifically proven, that acid prevents poisoning on the contrary may cause more problems in your health if you inhale excessively, it is best to use a gas mask and set fire every 50 cm (19.7 inches) that is excavated, in case there is gas this is consumed.

If you were able to find the treasure, you have to allow it to run and stay away from it, in addition to keeping the masks for at least 2 hours to avoid possible future poisonings.

How not to look for Treasures

Alone: Although the search for treasures is something that is enjoyed a lot in solitude unfortunately the times are not to do it that way. It is recommended to search accompanied by people of confidence.

In private property: If you do not have the permission of the owner of the property or land can be attacked since you can be considered a malicious intruder.

Unprotected: Gloves, Boots, Gas Mask, Cap and a first aid kit are some of the essential accessories for finding treasures when you go to places that are not very urbanized.

49

Code of Ethics for treasure seekers.

- Respect public and private property, as well as historical and archaeological sites, process or request the necessary permits.

- Respect local and federal laws regarding the search for Treasures.

- Do not cause damage to any type of property including fences, signs and buildings still in a situation of abandonment.

- Always fill the excavated holes.

- Do not leave litter or other junk objects found.

- Bring all the extracted rubbish objectives and deposit them in the corresponding deposits.

50

Final comment

Now that we know the concepts, places and basic techniques to start the search for the treasure, we can go to the field to start the search. We must mention that patience is one of the attributes that the treasure hunter must have, things of real value. you will find them from 100 hours of field experience.

Do not be disappointed if in your first searches and findings all you find are "worthless" things, corcholatas, nails, cans, etc. The experience is what will give us the desired results, so continue and continue searching, you will see that over time your performance as a treasure hunter will have had great improvements.

The value of things is not only in the type of metal therefore it is recommended to keep everything you find and investigate its value, whether historical or commercial, maybe you found your gold in copper.

Bibliography

- Hoja de datos técnicos de la bobina de exploración, http://www.garrett.com/hobbysite/hbby_searchc oil_tech_sheet_sp.aspx fecha de consulta: 11 de mayo de 2017
- Garrett Electronics, Inc. Manual de usuario ACE 400i, 2016. PN 1534300.A.0216
- Código Civil Federal, Libro Segundo, Titulo Cuarto, Capitulo III, Art. 875 al 885
- Fisher Research Labs, Inc. Manual de usuario F75, 2011
- http://www.garrett.com/hobbysite/hbby_faq_sp.aspx Fecha de consulta: 11 de mayo de 2017
- https://es.wikipedia.org/wiki/Detector_de_metales Fecha de consulta: 11 de mayo de 2017
- http://www.geosalud.com/ambiente/mercurio.htm Fecha de consulta: 12 de mayo de 2017
- http://norma-ohsas18001.blogspot.mx/2014/12/el-mercurialismo-o-hidrargirismo.html Fecha de consulta: 21 de abril de 2017

- https://www.ecured.cu/Metales_no_ferrosos
  Fecha de consulta: 17 de mayo de 2017
- https://www.textoscientificos.com/mineria/materiales-ferrosos Fecha de consulta: 17 de mayo de 2017
- Contreras, Vicente. Secretos de la localización de Tesoros. 11ª. Ed. 1986, Vicova Editores, ISBN 968-6218-07-6
- Rangel, Efrain, El culto de Nuestra Señora de Huajicori, Tesis de doctorado, Zamora, El colegio de Michoacán, 2008,273.

How to start in the search for Treasures?
Basic Information for beginners

Lic. Irving Jorge Galindo Salto

Gs Consultor

1st Edition May 2017

54

Irving Jorge Galindo Salto

How to start in the search for Treasures?
Basic Information for beginners

Irving Jorge Galindo Salto

55